Diamond Bars 2

Diamond Bars 2

poems
by David A. Romero

~ 2024 ~

Diamond Bars 2
© Copyright 2023 David A. Romero
All rights reserved. No part of this book may be used or reproduced in any manner whatsoever without written permission from either the author or the publisher, except in the case of credited epigraphs or brief quotations embedded in articles or reviews.

Editor-in-chief
Eric Morago

Editor Emeritus
Michael Miller

Marketing Specialist
Ellen Webre

Proofreader
Jeremy Ra

Front cover art
Julio Labra

Author photo
Damon Casarez

Book design
Michael Wada

Moon Tide logo design
Abraham Gomez

Diamond Bars 2
is published by Moon Tide Press

Moon Tide Press
6709 Washington Ave. #9297
Whittier, CA 90608
www.moontidepress.com

FIRST EDITION

Printed in the United States of America

ISBN #978-1-957799-20-9

Further Praise for Diamond Bars 2

Back with the follow-up to his 2010 *Diamond Bars: The Street Version*, David A. Romero maintains his focus on the Southern California landscape in *Diamond Bars 2*. The speaker in these poems confesses as much as he proclaims, with internal struggles that burst from the edges of lines. In some ways, this collection is a quest for comfort within one's own city and culture; in others, Romero's speaker's attempts arrive at his own story, both within and outside his Diamond Bar, upbringing, and everything else he's inherited. In these poems, Romero extends himself. Creative and muscular— Romero's is a hand reaching across the stage toward the audience.

— Michael Torres, author of *An Incomplete List of Names: Poems*, Creative Writing Fellow: National Endowment for the Arts, 2019

Those of us who have lived in greater Los Angeles will identify what David A. Romero is talking about immediately in *Diamond Bars 2*. In some ways, these towns are unlike anywhere in the world, and Romero captures the energy and tedium and difficulty there with beauty. In other ways, Diamond Bar, CA is like every other city in the United States, and Romero captures the inherent contradictions and pains and joys of that too. Romero brought me back to the Pomona Valley with each poem. His work moves me.

— John Brantingham, author of *Life: Orange to Pear*, poet laureate of Sequoia and Kings Canyon National Parks

David A. Romero's *Diamond Bars 2* is a phenomenal seasonal cycle- -a memoir of poetry that simultaneously delivers the raw honesty of the outsider while doing a deep dive inside the geography of the heart and culture of place and history.

— Margaret Elysia Garcia, author of *Graft, Burn Scars,* and *the daughterland*

Romero's poetry produces rumbling musical and emotional effects capable of bringing out previously unknown volcanoes of ideas, images, and makes us rethink our past, present and future.

— gabor g. gyukics, Beat Poet Laureate of Hungary, literary translator

*This book is dedicated to my sister Julie.
Thank you for taking me to the movies.*

Contents

Foreword by Kenneth Kirkeby   10

Spring

Bloom	16
The 286	17
Diamond Bars 2	21
Searching for Mexicans in Suburbia	25
The Day the Vests Played Ball	28
Mother Cuddler	32
Tall Cans on the Curb	35
You Were Born a Tree	39
Shovel	42
Silverado	43

Summer

Summer at the Movies	48
Bridalveil	52
Like Trying to Strike a Match Underwater	56
Suburban Problems	58
The Nuts	60
The Redemption of Roxy Salgado	64
This Way to the World's Greatest Merchants	69

Fall

Basketball with Edgar Allan Poe	78
A Safe Place to Live	81
A Neighborhood of Glass Houses	84
It Washes Us Away	87
Batman Rides Shotgun with Barbie	89
Bucky	92
Sean	95
Jeremiah	98

Winter

New Year's Day	102
I Wept and Howled that Night	104
I Am the One Who Knocks	106
In 30	109
Room 108	112
I'd Like to Be	114
Because I Could Not Stop for Money	115
Your Life is a Landscape	118
Familiar Ghosts	122
Say a Prayer for Me	123
About the Author	*125*
Acknowledgements	*126*

Foreword

Dear Reader,

As you open *Diamond Bars 2*, you are perhaps asking yourself: why would anyone write a book about Diamond Bar, California? Especially a book of poetry? Because, to the casual visitor, Diamond Bar, California, is not a particularly poetic place. Rather, it is a quite unremarkable suburban town—an amalgam of detached houses (packed closely together in hillside tracts), condos and apartments (packed closely together on canyon floors), and—on the highest hilltops, a sprawling gated community (The Country) of assertive, and occasionally bombastic, mansions. Though differing wildly in scale, most of Diamond Bar's buildings share a certain blandness in architecture—a kind of "nowhere" style wryly characterized in one of this book's poems as "Spanish/Dutch." Demographically, a similar ethnic inconclusiveness prevails: Chinese, Korean, Indian, White and/or Hispanic. Nothing too certain. Nothing too defining. In short, a lot of people live in Diamond Bar who feel more from elsewhere than from there.

All of this I know, because, for twenty years, I was one of those casual and vaguely alien residents. I lived in this town, but only because I worked there. Daily, I journeyed past its strip-malls and gas stations on my way to Diamond Bar High School—where I was employed as an English teacher, and where one year, as chance would have it, the writer of these pages—David A. Romero himself—turned up as a student enrolled in one of my honors English classes. I knew right away that a young man of David's intelligence and sensitivity was "a keeper." So, I kept him—at least as a social-media friend—and I have followed his subsequent life and career with great teacherly affection.

Coincidences, thus, comprise my modest qualifications for writing a foreword to *Diamond Bars 2*. I know the setting, I know the writer, and—once upon a time—I taught this writer poetry. Of course, I am not myself a poet, and even if I were, I woefully lack the "street cred" necessary to write about Diamond Bar—which I tended to regard, with the (unjustified) smugness derided in another of this book's poems, as little more than a "safe place" to live. David A. Romero, on the other hand, did choose to write about Diamond Bar, and he did so, I think, for two particularly compelling reasons: familial attachment and artistic detachment.

By "familial attachment" I am speaking metaphorically, of course, about a community and not a specific nuclear family. But I do wish to stress Romero's strong sense of belonging to an actual collectivity. Unlike me and many other "unassimilated" residents, Romero had (and continues to have) both a physical and an emotional relationship with his city. It is his—and he is an integral part and product of it, just as one is, for better or for worse, part and product of one's own family. Such a bond obviously transcends superficial considerations of "sights to see" or "things to do." Romero has embraced Diamond Bar, not uncritically, but with honest pragmatism, as a source of support and identity. Within its familial environment, this native son has matured and, in so doing, has sought autonomy and affirmation. Though that is a sometimes painful (albeit natural) evolution, throughout the entire process Romero has maintained a sincere devotion to his town, because, as he says in one poem, he prefers *familiar "ghosts."*

If Romero's emotional attachment is what gives passion to his words, it is his corresponding artistic detachment that affords him the distance and perspective necessary for cohesive thematic development. It is often said that good writers must step back from their subjects, judging them not only immediately and up close, but also through a wider lens and within a broader context. This is what Romero, with a filmmaker's eye, perceives. Recognizing that, superficially at least, his town often merits the joking epithet of "Diamond Bore," Romero has (I think) chosen to adopt a "big picture" view of his nondescript city—as a poetic protagonist in its own right. He sees, with his wide editorial lens, that the city's inchoate search for definition mirrors, in some sense, his own personal quest for identity and that, consequently, the city's own "groping" can serve as an overarching metaphor for the soul-searching manifested by the speaker who narrates all the poems of *Diamond Bars 2*.

Romero chooses to organize the collection's discrete poems in such a way as to present a loose, picaresque story of a protagonist (the speaker) on a series of encounters and conflicts that together constitute a journey of discovery and self-definition. The subheadings "Spring," "Summer," "Fall," "Winter," further suggest that, in Romero's mind, this journey has a kind of seasonal quality, like a yearly sequence— something not exactly final, but instead procedural— a cycle whose conclusion presages a new beginning and a continuation of the process.

Perhaps the interplay of familial attachment and artistic detachment is most compellingly presented via the metaphor that both opens and closes *Diamond Bars 2*: riding a regional bus. After a short scene-setting poem, the principal narrative begins with a poem entitled "The 286" in which the speaker finds himself on the number 286 bus, seemingly a bit confused about where he is headed, both physically and psychologically—toward Pomona or Brea—toward this feeling, or that fantasy. His tentativeness underlines the themes of youthful indirection and indiscretion which prevail throughout the early subsections of this collection—*Spring* and *Summer*. But the collection's narrative ends, fittingly—after the turmoil of *Fall* and *Winter*—on the very same number 286 bus, this time with a more self-assured speaker bound for a destination clearly outside of Diamond Bar and clearly beyond his initial Diamond Bar identity.

Here, though, as always, his love for his hometown endures: he has internalized this place just as surely as this place has served him as a crucible in which his better self has taken shape. He therefore expresses heartfelt thanks to his mother city, and pleads with it, as one would plead with a mother, to "pray for him" as he ventures outward. Though he regrets his own missteps, he acknowledges that he has grown positively over the course of this metaphoric, year-long journey. I think that the speaker's awareness, at this point, is that of the native son and the poet conflated, a savvy blend of both emotional attachment and artistic detachment. Thus, with momentary hyper-awareness, the speaker confesses to a sense of "selfishness" regarding the hometown that he must now, in his new autonomy, often leave behind. Still, return visits will surely occur, and Diamond Bar will surely abide as both a physical and spiritual home base. Thus, as another poem fervently insists (in Romero's own voice), this proud poet remains ever prepared, in defense of his hometown, to spit, "Bars of Diamond."

— Kenneth Kirkeby
English and French Teacher, *Retired*
Diamond Bar High School

Spring

Bloom

By the time the flowers bloom
You won't appreciate them.

The 286

These were the years of the 286
Whirring motor and compressed air
Refuge and wait
The limbo between worlds
Paid my way with bills and change
Three cities
Two counties
Connected
One
A route northeast
To that community named after some ancient goddess
That near neighbor
Like border town
Like privileged kids slumming it
A place of everyday people
And everyday struggles
But for this passenger
Of danger and intrigue
A place for dreams
The second
To that county south
We once celebrated
The mall and the theaters
An air-conditioned heaven
Of casual dining and the promise of Disneyland
Not too far in the distance
And where should this bus take me to
But a seemingly dead-end job in the same city
Of dangerous machinery and physical labor
To side hustles in the early morning hours
To offices to sign countless documents
To pay bills for crimes that lingered and lingered?
A life caught between stops
Requested only by something broken
Or never fully functional in the first place
How long could I ride my life?

Stare at my phone or look through windows
Watching Pomona
Diamond Bar
Brea?
With their streetlights and street signs
Deep nights
And early yearnings pass me by?
And car riders
Those privileged enough
To have never relied on the 286
To have never waited on that train of an automobile
Chugging and whooshing
Would ask,
"How do you do it?"
"Isn't it dangerous?"
And each question
Illuminated like route marquee
Just how different
The lives of people
Intersected by route
Those who would never know bus
And those who would never know car
Because this is California
And public and transportation
Meet at different intersections
And should some experience
Unexpected hardship
Better
Perhaps
To commit white collar crimes
To consume prescription pills
Until you die
Anything to avoid the stench
Of passenger
The sharing of seat
The exchange of conversation
The abrupt confrontations
That could break out at an any moment
And no escape except

The next stop
A few blocks up
And who knows how long it could take
To get back on?
Or how hot or cold it would be
On the walk?
And you
I know you
You wrecked your car
Lost your license
But I still see you from the 286
Driving
Behind the wheel of something new
Because your money never knew penance
Your checking account never knew change
You borrowed more money from your parents
And had the nerve
To give me lectures
About how I needed to learn how to save
And for you riders still riding
I see you too
Sitting tight clutching purses
Earbuds in singing
Or quietly nodding
Those leaning over seats
Standing
Swaying
Engaging in impromptu interviews
Of your fellow passengers
Like it's your own late-night show
And though you would never admit it
This is the best your day is going to get
I promise I won't forget
When car riders and drivers
See measures on ballots
See funds proposed towards transit
Lament corruption
And euphemisms for what they think of your lives
I will vote "yes"

For the renovations
The seats
The heaters
The air-conditioners
The wheelchair access
The bike rack
The wheels
The motors
May they carry you
And ferry you to your destination
Because the 286
Connects these cities
With a whirring motor and compressed air
You may ride it someday
Looking at the schedule
Anxiously awaiting
Gazing at road, anticipating
Future's arrival.

I wish you well on your journey.

Diamond Bars 2

You know what they say about home, right?
You know, aside from, "Home is where the heart is?"
And "There's no place like" it?
They say, "You can never go back"
Well…
What if you never left?

The buried farm of Spadra
The paved Diamond Bar Ranch
The 57 and the 60
These are the lifestyles
Of the Allegros and The Country
The bike ramps of King Kong
The ghosts of Brea and Carbon Canyons
The cut-down nogales trees
The windmill that still stands
The sticky seats of the Krikorian
White-boarded back issues at Comics N' Stuff
The thick and translucent covers
Of VHS tapes at On-the-Go Video
Polaroids of birthday celebrations
Complete with sombreros and maracas
At The Whole Enchilada
My friend Aaron Gutierrez's skater soul
That died the day
He broke his board in half in front of Trinity Board Shop.

Now, I'm talking about older times
Back when kids were still mean
Knew dirt
Blood
And trouble
Skateboards and bikes
Cigarettes and knives
But what do I know?
I spent most of my time as a youth inside

Reading novels when my classmates
Were still reading picture books
I knew I was destined to leave this place
Become someone great
My domain would never be Oak Tree's lanes
The scuffed bowling balls spinning in the gutters
Happy's Grille
The wanderers
From bus stop to bus stop
Because Diamond Bar
Was my family's moving-on-up
Our *Far and Away*
Our homestead at the edge of nothing
Now, pushing
Further and further east
This was our model minority
Anti-public swimming pool majority
Two-hundred grand
Made million offers in cash
Opportunity
But that's my parents' success story
And not mine
And each time
I leave this town
It's not long enough for it to miss me
I'm still hoping for a parade
The keys to the city
But, what
Beyond absence
Could make the heart grow fonder?
Maybe the maple leaves of Champlain, Vermont?
Spokane's falls?
And Walla Walla's creeks?
The shores of Lake Michigan?
The Rocky statue in Philly?
Arms high
Roaring applause
The flyers?
The posters?

The recorded interviews?
International reviews?
Dinners with university presidents?
And hotel suites?
Breakfast in dozens of towns
With patrons capping their nights
And starting their days in
Airports and bus stations?
Searching the pixels of schedules
To find their way?

But in every bus
Car window
And plane
I think about going back to the place…

Diamond Bar
The suburban city
Snoop Dogg lives in
The streets
My sisters drove their first cars on
The church garage and pantry
My mother gave out donations from
The basketball court
Where my brother beat NBA forward Keith Van Horn
The gyms
Where my father coached youth teams
To buzzer-beating victory
The city newspaper
Where a story on this poet once loomed larger
Than two-time Olympic gold medalist Alex Morgan's
And yeah, I know there's a big difference
Between "local"
And "legend"
But I'm on my way to being both
This is my city
This is my home
And to anyone still asking,
"Who is this dude

And why is he rhyming?"
Well, my name's David
Mr. Romero to some of you suckas
And I still spit
Bars of Diamond.

Searching for Mexicans in Suburbia

I still rue the day my white friends
Held my culture up to a magnifying glass
Thought they had learned enough about Mexicans
And "real" Mexican culture
They could tell me our hometown Mexican restaurant was fake
And I was fake for liking it
And that is something I will never apologize for
Because no matter how kitschy
A Mexican restaurant in suburbia is a sanctuary
A safe space
A place one goes to hear corridos
Surround oneself with beautiful colors
To smell fresh onion and chile and cilantro
To see and hear people who look like us
Even if they don't look like us
To have some comfort in knowing we're with fellow Mexicans
With all of that
So-called
"Outdated"
Norteño Spanish mission design
That the hipsters and Chipsters hate, alike
To remember a time
When this land was ours.

It was always implied
Or stated outright
By our classmates and our neighbors
We didn't belong here
We weren't white
Weren't Asian
They were the mostly affluent
Majority populations
And we were middle class
To struggling
Ahedo
Acosta

Martinez
Gonzalez
Valenzuela
Hernandez
Carrillo
I could count on my fingers
The Spanish surnames
Of kids from my classes
(The ones that didn't belong to Filipinos)
And by high school
You were given a choice of being "real"
And only hanging out with your own
Or being "white" or "weird"
Either was thought of as better
Than being a gardener
Landscaper
Housekeeper
Busboy
These were the people that held up to outsider scrutiny as,
"Real Mexicans"
It was both the deep shame
And the overwhelming pride
I say,
If you're searching for Mexicans in suburbia
Then look no further!

But if you want to hold our position here
Up to a magnifying glass
You might not be happy with what I find
You're an expert on the history of my hometown?
Come at me with tales of the Diamond Bar Ranch?
Like I don't know that the word cowboy
Comes from caballero?
Like I don't know that rock and country
Are played on a Spanish guitar?
Like I don't know that this land was once
Rancho San Jose y Rancho Los Nogales?
Combining to make up for most of the current cities of
Brea

Pomona
Diamond Bar
West Covina, Claremont, and Walnut?
These cities have names in Spanish
Anglicized Spanish names
Because they were once owned by Mexicans.

Tacos Azteca
Taco Factory
Paco's Tacos
La Olla
The Whole Enchilada
Each loss has been crushing
But even then
Our presence is strong in
La Puente
West Covina
Pomona
And Ontario
Growing
Not just restaurants
But dance studios
Cultural and art centers.

Each base
We have lost
Shall be regained!
Because here
In Southern California
Mexicans predate suburbia
And here we shall remain.

The Day the Vests Played Ball

Today the Vests play ball
An outfield and diamond
Of dirt and dust
Pebbles and concrete
The Vests take the field in a city junkyard
As the Uniforms watch them from their trucks
The Vests
Court-ordered
Community service workers
Everything from first-offense
First-timers
To multi-offense
Seasoned veterans
Men and women
Who have spent more time in the neon mesh Velcro
Than out of it
The city employees call them, "Vests"
The meaner ones call them, "Inmates"
Whether in the vans or outside
They say
To remind some
Where they've been
To tell some
Where they're going
Some days
The Uniforms like to gesture as they drive by State,
"Don't you worry
Some of you will be in there
Soon enough"
They find this
Hilarious
Most Vests immediately respond,
"Ah
Hell
No!"
Some Vests reflect quietly

As they drive by that complex
Of concrete
Field
And fence
Thinking they're just glad to be out
Others
Usually sitting right by the door
Or all the way in the furthest corner of the back
They gnash their teeth
They've got an itch in their blood
They curse the Uniforms
Under their breath
And the anger stays with them
Long after they get out of the van…

On lunch break
We vests chew on clouds of dust
Like all the bitterness of the past
Like the fear that we're not actually all innocent here
That all this time costs a lotta money
That we have some serious shit to deal with
And that something's gotta give
Or it won't
And we'll spend a lot of time chewing on that
Or we won't
But not today…
No.

Today, the vests play ball!
A broken broom
Or shovel handle for the bat
Pizza box and traffic signs for the bases
Fast food burger wrappers for the ball
We don't need gloves to catch with
We have our hands
Today the Vests play ball
Moises is on first
Guillermo is on second
Antoinette is on third
Cullen is up to bat

And I'm at the pitcher's mound
Serving up soft balls because
Who doesn't want to see
These Vests run the bases in this junkyard like champions?
We try
To make those burger wrappers fly
We run
Our open Vests wave like banners
We steal bases
And joke with each other
Those too embarrassed
Or too tough to play
They tease us from the benches made bleachers
The city employees come around
They ask each other,
"Are those inmates playing baseball?"
They laugh,
"Looks like they're playing with a bunch of trash!"
We're just a bunch of trash-people to most of them
Because their world is made up of rules
The dirty and the clean
The good and the bad
Purchased equipment
And piles of dirt
Dirt
That only children and idiots
Would choose to shape into tunnels and sandcastles
Forgetting that no game would exist without some nutcase
Having put sticks
Balls
Baskets
And lines in the sand together
To create
Sport
A city employee remarks,
"Looks like they're having fun"
"Well, why don't you join them, then?"
And he does
Comes up for a hit

Makes it
Smiles
and leaves
The ball falls apart
The game ends as unceremoniously as it started
Lunch is over
The Vests get back into the van
Some Vests leave
Others come in
But every time we pass by that junkyard
I'll tell them
About the day the Vests played ball.

Mother Cuddler

She said I dressed like a gentleman
And from the moment she grasped me
I held her hand
Lifted her feet over rain gutters and puddles
Like her protector
Her prince charming
My smile proves disarming at times
And her smile was full of promise
We rampaged through Downtown
Full of booze
Filling the pavement and air
With shouts and laughter
Loud and reckless
We owned the night like we were throwing bricks
And knocking over lampposts with our walk
She talks like she knows me already
Licks her lips
Like she's ready to party
We drink some more
She pulls me into a dark corner
Made for confessions and secrets
Tells me how glad she is for this moment
Her tattoos talk of rejection
Single-motherhood
And ovarian cancer at far too young of an age
She's hurting inside
Rockabilly-look-tough
All an illusion
Tears stream from her eyes
"My father died from cancer,"
I say
I can relate
She holds me
She collects wounded dogs
Seems like I've picked up a stray myself
Real hard luck case

We cling to each other
Like we were made for each other
But we don't belong together
After all, I'm a nice guy
And she's complicated
With lots of problems
I hope that I'm going back to her place tonight
We lie in her bed
I lie in her bed
Tell her how I can't wait to see her again
And how it's ok
That we're snuggling
Cuddling
When we could be—
But, we need this
I hold her head close to me
So she can feel my heartbeat
Desperate
Like she's the teddy bear
As a little boy, I cried into
She is the mother tonight, I will cry into
She says,
"You must really like me,"
I don't
And I'm sorry
Because I'm supposed to be a nice guy
Years ago, my father died
Single mother
You, are dying
You lay me down to sleep
I will awake before the coming of the morning
Pull myself from your embrace
And a tangle of sheets
Single mother
You forgive me with your longing eyes
And weary smile
My coat hangs heavy
My tie strangles
I leave

Walking through your open door
Filled with regrets
I know
I will never mean to see you again.

Tall Cans on the Curb

There
In front of that house on Lanfranco
Where the smell of musty wood pours out from the house
Where birds chirp from electrical wires
Where "Turkey in the Straw" radiates in the distance
Not too far from where I sat with the neighbor's kid
On a visit to my Grandfather's
And we watched the 1960s Batman
On a blurry jury-rigged antenna-wire television—

My dad and his neighbor from that same house
Sat with their beer cans on the curb when they were teenagers
And when my dad finished his sobriety
After years without
And a diagnosis the opposite of remission
My dad and his friend bought tall cans from the corner store
And drank on the curb there in front of their childhood homes.
They offered up cheers to better times.

I drank 40s with my friend
On the driveway of my parents'
Piles of cigarette butts and empty cans between us
And when the 5-O rolled up with flashing red and blue
I told my friend to chill out and remain seated
I was sitting there cross-legged, cross-faded
The smell of skunk still lingered in the air
When I told the officers, "I live here. This is my property."
Sometimes it seems like those were the best times...

See, I am a deacon in the Brotherhood of Tall Cans
My friend, a card-carrying member of the Curb Drinker's Club
The 40s and Four Loko High Society of
Concrete and Liquid Courage
We aren't just known alcoholics
To anyone within earshot of our stories
We're infamous

Just because we gather mostly inside
Mostly under the cover of night
Why should we hide?

We are the cheers
We are the toasts
We are the swirl
We are the suds
Of barley and rye
Of stomach acid
Ferment
And piss
The piss leaking down our legs
The piss pouring from our sweat
The smell of piss
On our breath
And their upturned noses!
Who are they to judge us?

We are the toilets
The porcelain gods
Vomit-filled and unforgiving
The bathroom faucets
Always thirsty
We are the bottles
Never quite filled
Always empty
We are the insults
We are the violence
We are the pounding
We are the blood
And we are the lies we tell our blood
I was the water, glucose, and sodium
Falling from my mother's eyes
Before I could finally stop.

My father lies in his casket
After losing his battle to cancer
The mortician has sculpted his mouth

So that he'll look happy forever
My sisters, my brother, and I gather
Into the rose-colored viewing room of the chapel
Looking at our father's wrinkled, placid, and powdered smile
We joke about tucking cans of beer into his coat
For him to be buried with
Like we did with our uncle.

I get hammered the following weekend
Then hammered by fists
By a friend
In front of our friends
In a campground in the desert
Screaming
Wailing
Imagining myself inside my father's casket
I imagine myself as him
I imagine myself being buried with him.

The morning after
I look into a mirror
Both eyes swollen and blackened
I resemble a raccoon.

A few days
Or months into sobriety
After my second DUI and losing my license
I walk along a curb in my city
And on my way home
I start singing
The words come to me suddenly,
"For years I drank to remember my father
But it won't bring him back
No, it won't bring him back
For years I drank to forget my problems
But he wouldn't've liked that
No, he wouldn't've like that."
I cry as I repeat it
Probably sounds corny if you haven't lived it

I shy my eyes from the oncoming traffic
As I sniffle, I smell the
Chlorine from a nearby apartment complex's pool
And I stop to watch the birds flitting
From the branches of eucalyptus trees lining Grand Avenue
That smell of musk and mint.

You Were Born a Tree

You were born a tree
A tiny seedling
In a bustling world
Yearning to break free
You were born a tree
Roots behind your growth
Branches glowing in sunlight
You were born a tree
Breathing in the badness
Of the bustling world
Producing something beautiful
Bright green leaves
Fruit for the future
In a time of deforestation
You were born a tree
Dragged before a machine
First a pile then
Arranged single file
Line of orders
Line of business
Line of march
Next
They cut off your arms
Which had once stretched with hope and promise
Towards many directions
You were going to be the first
Veterinarian-Astronaut-
Firefighter-Doctor-Truck Driver-tree
This all made perfect sense to you
You were going to stretch
Those branches towards the light
But your branches were cut
And the traces sanded down and polished smooth
You were given
One direction to grow in
Your designated shape

Inches in diameter
Thin and uniform
Your head affixed
With a mind of metal ideas
The kind that makes you think,
"I know who I am
I know what I am
I have worth
I have value
I like myself
Because
I am a hammer
And it's great to be a hammer
Because I live in a world full of nails"
WHACK
WHAM
BANG
Everything looks one way
You begin to feel hatred and distaste
Towards anyone who ever suggested
That trees were meant
To be trees
Branch out into the sunlight
Make their own leaves
Those around you
No longer beautiful trees
They are tools
Purposed
Some became shovels
Some brooms
Some pencils
Some scythes
Some rulers
Some hoes
Some were discarded
Never given a head at all
In this bustling world
Some are saying,
"One head isn't enough"

That it was foolish to affix tools
With only one
They say
Tools were meant
To resemble pocketknives
A jumble of metal
Ugly heads stabbing in all directions
Almost like branches stretching towards the sun...
But the more heads
And the more tools
Seems like fewer and fewer are of use
More and more discarded
Some tools question
"What did we do?
How can we be used?
What I wouldn't do for another head
I would break other tools
I am a tool
I have a purpose
I am not worthless!"
Maybe in your desperation
Depression
In their condemnations
You have forgotten
That you were made a tool
But you were born a tree
A tiny seedling
In a bustling world
In this refuse and dirt
Your branches sprout
Flimsy and weak
But they can link
You can grow again
You can be whole again
You were born a tree.

Shovel

It's ok if you dig yourself into a hole
Just make sure to never bury your shovel
And if you suggest that you'll dig
Whether in or out
With your hands
All the working world will know,
You've never actually done too much digging,
Have you?

Silverado

The warehouse seemed to get a little brighter
Whenever she walked in
She brought in beams of light with her
Beams that made her too bright to look at directly
Beams so bright
They illuminated the boxes and cases
The dirty blue and yellow steel
The stacks of pallets piled over you those afternoons
The four corners
The shrink rap
The barking orders
To get done on time
Do it faster
Do it right
There she would enter
With her orange platform cart
Her wavy hair flowed like the giant cape of a queen
Dolled up with full makeup
Tank top and ripped jeans
But conversations made her uncomfortable
Co-workers all thought she was stuck-up
Because she didn't really enjoy stopping
To talk to them or anyone
Cinthia worked for her mother and father
And that full figure
Was supported by a full frame
She didn't want
Or ask for
Your help
But you gave it to her anyways
It took you weeks
Maybe even months
To work up the courage to ask her for her name
Even after you had loaded her silver Silverado
Outside
Grunting

Dripping sweat in that truck bed
Hoping your labor might one day get you into another
You were friendly with her mother
And kind enough to her father
And when she started working full-time for them
And dressing down
With her hair in a ponytail
Tucked under a baseball cap
You saw it as your opportunity
You didn't exactly sweep her off her feet
But each exciting first eventually came
Those first orders at their restaurant counter
Became the first time operating the register
And you found yourself
Proving your devotion and loyalty
By working for her family
You lost track of who was doing who the favor
You didn't care
There was only your love
For Cinthia
Mi linda Cinthia
You were a Don Juan of the dishes
A Shakespeare of order-pulling
A Cyrano de Bergerac of taking out the trash
And now
As you stand at their register
Wiping the steel and tile counters
For the millionth time
Checking the levels of the agua frescas
Gazing towards the light coming in from
The full glass entrance
You watch Cinthia come in
And she no longer brings in beams of light with her
Only resentment
Towards her parents
Towards this job
Towards that bar that had to close down
Where she had once trained and worked as a bartender
Where she would much rather have spent her afternoons

With men and women who could have offered her jewels
Ranches
And horses
As she smiled
Sprinkled salt
And arranged the garnishes for their glasses
And it all would've been much better
Than these hours and sweat
And your sense of humor
That stupid sense of humor
That once made her laugh
Stop
And talk to you.

Summer

Summer at the Movies

You should've seen this place when it was new
The glass on the admissions booth
Was spotless
The doors covered with posters
Stickers
And cut-outs for new releases
And when you opened those doors
A wave of fresh popcorn greeted your nostrils
Turn left
There's concessions
Turn right
The arcade alley
When they brought in games
Each was an event
The talk of the town
The type of thing to make you wish you could
Conjure another quarter from your pocket
And beyond
The T-section
That led to where the magic really happened
The ticket counter
With the girl my older brother had a crush on
Bright-eyed and braced-faced Jackie
Pony-tailed
In immaculate uniform with bright copper name badge
Ushered you in with a warm greeting
That was when the floors were clean
When all the seats folded up properly
Before the upholstery was covered in gum and torn
Before much bigger theaters opened
Just miles away
Before businesses in that same shopping center shut down
There was definitely something in the air that summer.

But all the better for us
The moviegoers
Between middle and high school
Adolescence and adulthood
Tara and Ignacio
Were my best friends
Had been
Since the theater was brand new
This was the perfect place for us
Close enough to walk or ride our bikes to
Somedays
Tara would come over
After practices at Ina Dance Studio
The theater was a place we could stop in
For a game or two
Or spend entire afternoons in
Watching those images flicker across the screen
To the steady hum of the projector
We'd buy a ticket
Or sometimes
Just candy or a drink
Sneak past the now empty ticket counter
Head into the next one
We watched whole movies
Sometimes just pieces
Ones we knew the dialogue to
And new releases
Sometimes Tara would stand up on a chair
Half of her body lit by the image
Her shadow cast upon the screen
She'd shout
Re-enact a scene from the movie
"Nacho" was the ringleader
The one who showed us
How to move from theater to theater
He'd learned how to do it from his older sister
Who'd stopped going to the theater a long time ago
That summer of mundane magic
Of the sticky spots on the floor

That made our shoes squeak
They greeted us like old friends
That summer we would leave in evenings
That were still warm
At first
Twilight more of a suspicion
Than a reality
And months later
"It's getting dark out"
Still meant it was time to head home
We each had nights that summer
Tara's dad
Ignacio's mother
My dog Ginger
When we didn't want to leave the theater
Urged the others to stay
To watch another one
The air was still ripe then
Sometimes
Fights
Someone pulling a knife
High schoolers having sex
40s and weed
Played in our theater as coming attractions
One day we arrived,
And the doors were closed
A notice posted on the glass
Framed in clear tape,
"Changing ownership"
The admissions booth and theater were dark
The projectors inside
Still and silent
"Nacho" was the first to leave
His father had a new job in a county or two over
Tara and I had moments
We held hands
Even kissed a couple of times
But really
Had different interests

Found different cliques
You wouldn't have known
What we had once meant to one another
If you had seen us walk by each other
In the hallways of our high school.

That winter
When they finally opened the doors to the theater
Just to clear everything out
I heard from one person
That when they went inside
And shone their flashlight on one of the walls
There was a silhouette
Behind where one of the movie screens used to be
They said it was a perfect black silhouette of a girl
In a dancer's pose.

I guess it was just a little reminder
Of that summer at the movies...
Before The Krikorian shut down.

Bridalveil

You can't believe it
Hopping rocks
Sure each foot
Will meet
On even surface
So, ankle stays steady
So, muscles can spring you
From one to the next
These rocks
These boulders
Are increasingly wet
Slippery
Some covered in moss
As the water
Clear
Trickles
Streams
And surges below
Your father is behind you
He calls out for you to watch out
To slow down
And you do
If only for a couple of seconds
You are enfolded in pine and canyon
Shaded by these monuments
The sky is an afterthought
What you're after
Is that surging monolith
A skyscraper of nature
That waterfall dominating your sight
Each time
You look up
Its thunderous crashing
Pounding your ear drums
Your view is obscured
By boulders the size of houses

Guarding its base
Eroded by millennia into jagged forms
They protect its secrets
And you want to know
The rocks can't be walked across
Or even jumped anymore
They have to be climbed
You lose your feet for a moment
Reach a handheld
Scrape skin
And find it
And the fear hits you
Like maybe this is too much
Like maybe you should turn back
In the distance
You can hear your father
Telling you the same
But you don't listen
It's calling
The sound of the foot
No longer obscured by its lesser offspring
It calls to you
You picture something perfect at its base
Something colorful and enchanting
A golden light, a rainbow through the foliage
And maybe some dinosaurs
And now
Breathless and exhausted
You pull yourself over those last pockmarked hurdles
And what you see
You can't believe
A world of gray
Of undulating mist
And stark contrasts
A world of
Jagged
Soaked
Rocks
Formed like an amphitheater

And at the main stage?
A pillar of white water
Like the trunk of a tree that could reach into space
Or the face of some mysterious and malevolent being
The pool surrounding its impact
Surprisingly small in circumference
Not a foot of tranquil water within it
Your only route
A slope
Of slippery brown megalodon teeth
To where this ancient goliath
Pounds down
With the weight of a mountain upon the earth
You realize you've made a terrible mistake by coming here
But still
You hear it calling,
"Come
Climb on down
Come to me
Let me crash over you"
It calls with certain death
And you
Climb further down
To wonder
If it really would take your life
And if so,
How quickly?
And now it lies
Assures you it will be fine
That its touch will feel like a gentle embrace
You know you have to leave.

The wet rocks are much harder to climb
Than they were to descend
But you make it
To a world of color
To smaller boulders
And lesser offspring
Pine and canyon

Nature that can fit into the palm of one's hand
And you feel joy again
See your father
He is relieved
Asks you what you saw
And you tell him
He nods his head solemnly
Says he was worried about you
Says to never do that again.

Bridalveil is still there
Among the wonders of Yosemite
Through day and night
It crashes
It still calls
Asks for you to return
Asks that you come under its veil
Asks that you stay
Floating in the water.

Like Trying to Strike a Match Underwater

Everyone knows about sparks
You spark a match
And once it's lit
Nothing can ever be the same
From friction to chemical reaction
A heat that spreads
On oxygen, it feeds
Changing anything in its path
Never to be the same
From dust to dust?
No, from form to ash
"Once I did that…"
They say,
"There was no going back"
And they all want to know about those single sparks
Those big bangs
"Let there be lights"
Inciting incidents
Story is a beautiful construct
Belying the limits of memory and perception
It's an interview
Of a limited truth
Like putting you into a room
Having you stare out of a window
And asking you to tell us what's going on in the world
Scientists say that the universe
Is just one bubble floating in a quantum foam
Jack Johnson sang that,
"All of life is in one drop of the ocean
Waiting to go home."

I remember how last summer I almost drowned
A lifeguard helped save my life
Laid out on a towel afterwards
On the verge of tears
Under a bright sun

Body still shaking
Still wet.

The context of my near-drowning
Defies all my carefully-constructed narratives
My near-drowning said nothing about my identity
And drowning was not something I had set out to do
I would not have died for my beliefs
Would not have died in the act of creation
I was on a family vacation
With a family I love
But often feel separate from
Sometimes these days
I get lost staring
Thinking about those waves crashing over my head
My distance from the shore
And the exhaustion setting in
And they say
That if I almost died that day
I must've learned something
There should've been some epiphany
Some new realization
But so far, it's been like trying to strike a match underwater
I know that most of the world is covered by water
And most of the universe is empty space
And the largest quantity of energy within it
Works as the opposite of gravity
Instead of pulling anything closer
It pushes everything away.

And what a sad ending to this story…

It's just like one bubble popping
In an infinite foam.

Suburban Problems

Shopping malls across America
Were covered in rock
Long slabs cut into decorative panels
Glued onto the faces of buildings
To give them color and texture.

Frank Lloyd Wright
Believed that in design
It was vital
To incorporate elements from the local environment
To make buildings
Appear as if they were just another part of the land's features.

Some of those new buildings were beautiful
Those rock slabs
Really did accomplish their stated goal
Of bringing more character
To those chain restaurants and big box retailers
But in the years between 2001 and 2006
My best friend
Neal
Didn't see decorative faces
He saw scalable ones
He didn't see walls
He saw handholds
Toejambs
Crags and footholds
Walls
Tall enough to give you a thrill
But not enough to take your life
Enough to break a leg or roll an ankle
But not enough to leave you paralyzed
From "bouldering"
The climbing of boulders
Neal called it "buildering"
The climbing of buildings

In rock climbing
The pre-charted set of moves
One can use to ascend a face is called a route
Each route has a scale of difficulty
Routes are also called problems
And problems started springing up all over suburbia
We drove in Neal's musty red jeep
With climbing shoes
Chalk bags and a green foam fold-up crash pad
Looking for them
One of our favorites was in Brea
An auto-repair shop
We only ever climbed it at night
Most of the time sober
But when Neal was drunk
No matter where we were
He would immediately take off
Start climbing the first thing he could see
He was reckless and fearless
Some people thought he was weird
Wanted to avoid him
But to some of us
He was a legend
Scale the face
Climb the mountain
Even if it's in your own backyard
Rock slabs with chalk marks already there
It was catching on
I started referring to it as a movement
The beginning of a suburban renaissance
Like bombing trains
Tagging walls
Grinding in empty pools
Businesses caught on
The faces were polished smooth
Smoother than the hardest routes on El Cap
And any remaining chalk marks
Were washed off
Wiped clean
Like the problems had never been there.

The Nuts

"You see these two cards?
How much you win or lose
Depends on how well you play them
You know the game
It's poker
Pairs and trips
Straights, flushes, and full houses
Raise case hands
Chase with rags
My advice
Make your hand right off the flop or fourth street
And ask for nothing from the river."

That was Ben
Teaching me how to play Texas Hold'em
It was the summer of 2006
And poker was in
Big money tournaments
Ruled the airwaves
And home games sprang up in living rooms
Dining rooms
Garages and backyard patios across America.

I got my first taste
In one such home game in Phillips Ranch
Seven/deuce off-suit
Became a straight-flush
$300 cash in beginner's luck.

Between games
I spent my days
Single and jobless
In front of the Hollywood Video
Where Ben worked
Hanging out with him during his breaks and lunch
With cigarettes

And a Nalgene bottle full of watered-down wine
Mid-afternoon
I would go in
Browse the titles
Eyes Without a Face
God Told Me To
Caligula
The covers alone haunted me
And sometimes Ben would ask
Why I didn't just rent them already
I'd tell him,
Like that line from the *The Shawshank Redemption*
"I think they're probably better in my mind."

Cameron
Our group's leader
Loved the ladies
Loved fights
One night
We had a standoff
With about fifteen guys
In a college parking lot
When we were only about eight or nine deep
I rapidly searched that parking lot for anything
I could use as a weapon
The Suicide King
I found some tire chains in the bed of a stranger's truck
Ben found me with them and wrestled them away
"If you bring these
One of them is going to get a gun!"
When he had heard what I had done
Cameron said I was nuts.

Cameron was knocked into a coma
At a backyard party a couple weeks later
Pounded by fists into a concrete patio
By a tatted-up white bro
In a black Affliction t-shirt
Slicked black hair and dead eyes

The bro sucker-punched a woman
And when Cameron jumped in
He took her place being pounded into the pavement
Ben and the others who went to help
Were punched or slapped off
By that bro like he was a superhuman
It was a good five minutes
Before someone finally called the cops.

It weighed on Ben for a long time
He told me about visiting Cameron in the hospital
Paused to take long drags of his cigarette
As he thought about it
His surprise
His regret
They weren't able to do more
I said nothing
Made excuses to myself
For why I had done nothing
I had been there that night, too.

By the river
Standing atop rocks we had once covered in graffiti
Ben asked me how I had been doing at poker lately.

I told him,
"I've been suffering a lot of bad beats…"
I stopped,
"You know what?
Actually
There were a lot of times I knew I was beat
But I went all-in anyways
You know what I mean?"

Ben said he did
Flicked his cigarette
We bumped our fists
He drove off
And in that same afternoon
He quit his job at Hollywood Video.

I applied
Got hired
Took it seriously
Folded up my poker table
Wrapped it in plastic
Put it in the garage
And after a few months of scanning tapes and DVDs
I had enough to buy a movie camera.

The Redemption of Roxy Salgado

"This seatbelt—
Is suffocating!
The walls—
They're closing in!"

These were the words of one Roxy Salgado
Of Rowland Heights, CA
Psychology student at UCLA
Before she unclicked her seatbelt
And opened her car door to the 10 Westbound
Psilocybin was pulsing through her veins
A whole bag of magic mushrooms churning in her stomach
Against the advice of members of her cohort
Three of them in that car
Couldn't manage to calm her down
Prevent her from tumbling out
Somersaults and side rolls
As her body went limp into the wind
The black pavement under the night's sky
Illuminated by post lights.

It wasn't Roxy's obituary
In the following morning's paper
But that of
Patricia Guzman
Mother of three
Resident of Pico Union, Los Angeles
Hailing from San Miguel, El Salvador
Severe trauma to her neck and spine
Blunt force trauma to her brain
From collision with dashboard
An airbag that never deployed
According to her husband Victor
Her last words were,
"Me duele"
"It hurts"

And fragmented questions
About the safety of their children.

Roxy awoke at a friend's house in Southeast Los Angeles
With a headache
Sprained ankle
Some cuts and bruises
Unanswered texts and voicemails
Clothes embedded with gravel
And stained with blood and vomit.

Three months later
Roxy is in a state between uppers and downers
Leaning on a chain-link fence
Across the street from a house in Pico Union, Los Angeles
It is once again nighttime
Roxy looks in through partially open windows
Revealing the Guzman family inside
Victor and his three children
There is laughter
There is screaming
There are long silences and muffled whimpers
Victor often walks around aimlessly
Moves to start something
And abruptly stops
The youngest of the three
Lusita
Has a Dora the Explorer doll
Sometimes she talks to it
Clutches it tightly for hours
Crouched in the same spot.

One month later
It is the eve of Lusita's birthday
Roxy has gathered that from outside surveillance
Roxy's parents
Have no idea she has functionally dropped out of school
Roxy spends most of her days visiting friends and dealers
Going to parties

Kickbacks
Afternoon hangs
Walking the lampposts and pavements of Los Angeles
But every trip eventually takes her back to the Guzmans
On one walk
Roxy found a discarded piñata on a curb
An unlicensed paper mâché and chicken wire
Dora the Explorer
That day Roxy picked it up
Took it with her on the bus and dragged it home
And fashioned it into a costume.

Roxy stands now
In the Guzman's kitchen with it on
After having broken in
Her mind is swimming
With uppers and downers
With guilt and hope
With the pain of something
That happened to her long ago
The little girl Lusita
Walks into the room
Sees her
As a shadowed paper mâché monster
And screams
Roxy lifts her costumed hands
To try and comfort Lusita
She wants to hold her for hours
Tell her everything will be ok
Lusita runs away
Continues screaming
Roxy hears rustling in other rooms
Victor shouts,
"Que es eso?"
Roxy panics
Tears the paper mâché head off
Sprints through the kitchen door
Through an alley
A block over

Roxy can still hear Lusita's terrified wailing
Roxy is panting and sweating
She leans on a fence still partially covered
In the collapsing costume
She weeps
As the neighborhood dogs
Awaken the neighborhood
One snaps behind her
Teeth colliding with the fence
Roxy runs
Eventually finding her way home.

Roxy never returns to the Guzmans'
She goes back to attending classes
Asks for extra credit
Graduates
And in time
Finds a job
On her best days
She forgets what happened
On her worst
She drinks
Pops pills
Starts doing something
And abruptly stops
Or sits for hours
In the same spot.

The Guzmans struggle with the loss of Patricia
For many years longer
Lusita occasionally awakens with nightmares
Of a paper mâché monster in the house
But in time
The nightmares abate.

Victor
Keeps a copy of the paper
On his antique wooden nightstand
With the article about what happened the night Patricia died

And within it
It outlines how Victor
Swerved into the shoulder of the freeway
To avoid a head-on collision
With a truck heading the wrong direction
There is a statement
Issued by the trucking company
Giving their most sincere condolences
Promising the immediate termination of the driver
And in the cold calculations of the value of Patricia's life:
The announcement of a settlement.

Nowhere in the article
Is given mention to a Roxy Salgado
Of Rowland Heights, CA
Or any other person
Who may
Or may not have been
In some way
Responsible
For the accident on the 10 Eastbound that night.

This Way to the World's Greatest Merchants

There's a shopping center in this town
And in that shopping center
(Clean and refurbished
With a design best described as Spanish/Dutch
Or beach chic
Some design scheme assembled by an architect
Hoping to capture the spirit of the city
Who eventually threw up their hands and gave up)
Is a corner coffeeshop
Once a franchise
Now independently-owned
And on that coffeeshop's shaded patio
Two friends
Both poets
Both writers
An unusual profession
In this town of schoolteachers and realtors
Sit and discuss their plans for the future.

One writer
So unsure
Or
Better yet to say
Sure of a grade of everything from stasis to calamity
The other
Sure of only toasts in towns seen and unseen
Of only haters that block the path
He gets out a book
Not to compose new prose or poetry
But to map out charts
Draw networks to climb
Projections of potential earnings
What an alluring web he weaves…

The moment broken
By barista offering free food as ruse to buy more

Samples of pastries set to expire soon
To be sold
But not on sale
"You wouldn't want us to throw this food away
Would you?"

Enter teenager
Baseball cap flipped to the back
Kicked up skateboard
Offers another opportunity
To help someone in need
He asks for a light
Then offers to trade cigarettes
One of the writers agrees
The teenager tells him
He should give him some money
In the exchange
After all
The teenager's cigarette
Comes from a more expensive pack
The writer concedes the point
Those are indeed
Quality cigarettes he has
The writer gives him a quarter
The teenager asks for another.

And who could forget
The businessman who parks his car in the spot
Right in front of where the two writers are sitting
When almost all the other spots are open?
The businessman is all smile and slick hair
Wristwatch and thin belt
But no tie or coat
Golf casual
To let potential customers know
Really
He's just like them
He once was lost
But now has found

Our Lord and Savior Jesus Christ
As well as personal and portable magnet massage devices
They're really just like one another
Always there for you
And capable of performing miracles
With powers unknown to science
Combine that
With some herbs from the old country
And you have medicine for whatever ails you
"You two
You seem like two smart guys
Two capable young men
I bet if you were to sell these devices
You could make a fortune
Believe me
When I came to this country
I had nothing
Been pulled into a scheme
What would I tell my wife and children?
I didn't have an answer
So, I went to church
And while there I met a representative for Triple M
Magnet Massage Messengers
And now
I've dedicated my life to only the Good News and positive ions!
You never know how going to church can change your life
Here
Why don't you give it a try?"
He shoves the vibrating magnets in the writers' faces
They wrinkle with displeasure
But before they can formally answer
The businessman spots a woman walking with a cane in the distance
"Ma'am!
Stop!
Let me heal you!"
He yells and gives chase
The two writers wonder if this isn't their cue to leave.

Enter scene
The king of the coffeeshop
The suburban dad
Who cosplays as beggar
And troubadour
For he is often accompanied by his guitar
He strums along mornings
Afternoons
And evenings
But never plays in professional settings
He is a white man with a full tan and hearty laugh
Every few generations
A cult of kids will surround him
Teenagers and college-aged young adults
To talk of all the goings-on in and around this town
Before they inevitably
Move on
Sometimes the king of the coffeeshop offers gossip
Historical tidbits
Or full-blown conspiracy theories
Involving some of the usual suspects:
UFOs and JFK
And then there was that strong anti-Islamic phase
But now
Everything is about the Chinese and the Japanese
About how they're "taking over"
"I'm not racist"
He says,
"I'm married to one of them!"
His live-in mother-in-law
Like rumors of Jack Ma and Alibaba
Always watching
Disputes over the branches of a neighbor's tree
Like Taiwan or Hong Kong
His wife and mother-in-law making financial decisions without him
Like Chinese bankers buying up lots in The Country
Upon which they will build their mega mansions
He often imagines the bricks
Beams

And stucco
Tumbling down the hills to fall down upon him.
"There is only one answer to all of this"
He says,
"And that is war!
It may be too late
But we can still move in
From Russia and the Philippines
Send in the troops
Rocket over the nukes!"
One of the writers has heard enough.

"There is only one country on Earth
That has used nuclear weapons
And that is the United States of America!
And if there's a country that needs
A pre-emptive strike launched upon it
It's the recidivist!"

Shouting follows
Personal insults
Fists pounding on the metal wire tables
Each man trying
Their damnedest
To sell the other.

Today is a unique day
Typically the king of the coffeeshop will have free reign
To play his jingle for any and all who will listen
And from those who drive down from The Country
To those who walk over from the apartments across the street
Many will agree with him
When it comes to the prospect of nuclear war
Parts of the town are utterly sold.

The other writer sits stupefied
Embarrassed by both men
But more by himself
He has always been something of a coward

Especially when at work
Or in his hometown.

Enter young college student
Says she recognizes the coward
From a feature in the local paper
She asks him if he's working on another book
He says he is
She asks him what it's about
He says,
"Well
It's about a lot of things
Privilege
Hardship
Loss
Nostalgia
The ghosts of the past
The beauty of our town
The pettiness of its people
The terror behind the veneer
The unyielding power of nature
A life on the road
The end of existence
And what it all might amount to"
He laughs and follows that up with,
"I don't know"
The college student doesn't appreciate his litany
Nor his false humility
She takes him to task,
"It doesn't sound
Like you have a good idea of what it's about
And you should really focus in on that
If you want it to be successful."

Here
Away from the hustle and bustle
The panic of freeways
The cutthroat of crosswalks and intersections
Here

Where life moves at a slower pace
Where people move for a taste of the pastoral
The American Dream with scattered palm trees
Track homes managed by sidewalks pristine
There's a shopping center with this coffeeshop in its corner.

But before you enter that shopping center
One can find a sign
A decades old wooden sign
Renovated and painted anew
Damaged from weathering
And multiple car accidents
The sign reads,
"This Way to the World's Greatest Merchants."

Fall

Basketball with Edgar Allan Poe

Dusk
Falls upon the basketball court
Airplanes loom overhead
Shooting hoops in loneliness
When all of a sudden
A strange thought drifts
Bump
Bump
Goes the basketball
Rapping upon the asphalt
What if this evening
I played basketball
With Edgar Allan Poe?

The poet appears suddenly upon the court
Dark and heavily-layered raven's cloth
Hardly the proper garb
Of a basketball player
Methinks
Still, he
Motions for the ball
And I pass it to him
He drives the lane
Towards the basket
And in desperation
I move to block him.

Edgar Allan Poe and I
Are playing a game now
Sweat and grit
Anger and determination
Win or lose
No draw
Bragging rights for eternity
And I've got all the advantage
That being alive
And a few good layups can allow.

But Poe posts up
Pump fakes his shots
In his wake
The backboard transforms
Into a swinging pendulum
Reminding me
That I have been playing in this pit
Of imagination and mundane reality
Long before I ever played against him.

Edgar Allan Poe is going to win
His every shot takes the air out of me
Inexplicably burying me alive
My smack talk is grave,
"You are dead, poet!"
"I am immortal"
Poe shoots the basketball
"You're just a zombie!"
I cry
"I am immortal"
Poe shoots the basketball.

"You are an emotionally disturbed nutjob
Weakling
Who should've been prescribed
Vicodin
Among other things
We put people like you
In looney bins!
You couldn't handle your alcohol
Your drugs
Your family
Your—
You need a probation officer
And a therapist!
Consumption

Took your incestuous wife from you
And you watched
Helplessly
Knowing there was nothing
You could do
To stop it…"

Poe
Never flitting
Still is shooting
"Pain and the terror of loss
Constitute my soul, poet
What are the contents of yours?"
He shoots
He scores
Forever more
Edgar Allan Poe retires from the floor…

At Dawn
I rise
To face his shadow
To be a writer
To be a poet
And
At long last
Peruse those volumes
Of forgotten lore.

Ladies and gentlemen
Edgar Allan Poe is immortal
That's why
One night
I let him beat me
At basketball.

A Safe Place to Live

This is a safe place to live
Windows without bars
Fences
Walls
Gates
Hedges
Hills
And distance
From any highly populated city
This is a safe place to live
Top-rated schools in the country
Friday night football games
Town center
With programs for seniors and children alike
This is a safe place to live
In this city
We fear no earthquakes
Fear no neighboring wildfires
Nor housefires contained to a house or two
We laugh at memories of our most infamous local gang
And the stabbings
Beatings
And muggings
They once perpetrated in this city
We do not fear our past
We do not fear the overgrown haunted cemetery of Spadra
Spotted from the 57
Engulfed by the trees
That once fit tightly between the headstones
We do not fear ghostly balls of light in Carbon Canyon
As children
We feared urban legends
Like those my sister's high school boyfriend
Cody
Told me
Of men who had escaped from Chino State Penitentiary

Men who roamed the tall weeds in the dead of night
Men who had hooks for hands
Or were missing an eye
Kid's stuff
That kind of thing doesn't happen here
This is a safe place to live.

Richard Ramirez
Claimed one of his victims
And assaulted another
August 8th, 1985
On Pinehill Lane in this town
Not too far from where I'm writing this now
A cul-de-sac
Full of one-story houses
A view of the San Gabriel Mountains
From the north side
That night
A last quarter moon hung in the sky.

November 2nd, 2018
A Diamond Bar native
Murdered his parents
And the family dog
Set the house ablaze
Before escaping into the hills
Friends and neighbors
Saw him roaming the streets of South Diamond Bar
In the weeks
Months
Years
Leading up to the murders
Troubled
But seemingly harmless
Another unfortunate victim
Of the onset of early 20s schizophrenia
We went to school together
Neal was once his next-door neighbor
Rumors abound his parents

Didn't believe in using antipsychotics to treat his illness
Perhaps they believed nothing could ever go wrong here
Everyone who lives here knows
This is a safe place to live.

Crooked Creek Drive
Is a street with two-story houses
With front-facing two-story windows
Like the eyes of sleepy and melancholy giants
Southbound on Crooked Creek
An opening to Brea Canyon
A waning crescent hung in the sky that night
As the curtains were set ablaze
Curtains
On windows
Like so many here.

A Neighborhood of Glass Houses

There's a street in this neighborhood
Much like any of the others
It's got one and two-story houses
Full of locked doors
And closed windows
They're houses of glass windows
With curtains held inches open
By delicate hands and suspicious eyes
Always scanning the street
For anyone and anything
Considered undesirable.

There's something new on this street
That has caught everyone's attention
It's a food truck parked on the corner
A taco truck
A rectangular prism
With bright colors
And bold fonts
It's parked in front of a neighbor's house
And most believe it doesn't belong here.

Everyone saw them move in not too long ago
That Hispanic family
A syllable or two away from something old
Familiar
But much too crass to say aloud
Really
They're not so different
Mostly quiet
Mostly keep to themselves
Live in their house with glass windows.

But that taco truck on the corner though
Is irregular
Is an eyesore

Must be against regulations
A homeowner's association
City ordinances
The neighbors agree
People must respect boundaries
Somebody must do something.

Neighbor Jane leads the charge
A hero with a landline
She calls up the Department of Public Works
Just a stone's throw away
Asserts what an orderly street
Her and her neighbors live on
What a disturbance this taco truck has caused
Can it be towed?
Can someone from the city at least
Come out and take a look?
Gossip travels through whispers
A date is set
Anticipation builds
A city official is coming
The neighbors reckon
This will be a day of reckoning.

The city official arrives
Turning the corner onto the street in this neighborhood
Passing the taco truck
Immediately noticing violations
One door down
A car permanently parked on cinder blocks on the lawn
Two doors down
Neighbors pouring chemicals into the storm drain
Three doors
Neighbors cut down a tree belonging to the city
Four doors
A retaining wall built without a permit
Five doors
Neighbor Jane receives five tickets

For five separate violations
The city official barely restrains himself
From writing on the back of one of Jane's tickets
An old phrase about throwing stones and glass houses
But that's all pretty common here.

The taco truck remains parked on the corner
The Hispanic family
Continues to live in the house on the street in this neighborhood
They live
Mostly quietly
Windows intact
Moving their taco truck only for business
And for the street sweeper on Thursdays.

And soon enough
They aren't the only Latinx family in the neighborhood.

It Washes Us Away

History is a river
Indifferent to our names
Our lives caught in its current
It washes us away.

Bev
Black hair and auburn eyes
Pale skin
Half-Caucasian by way of an estranged father
Half-Vietnamese by way of a single mother
And refugee grandparents.

My father was a Vietnam veteran
US Army
Artillery division
Loud booms and empty shells
Over lush fields and mountains
My siblings saw it as an act of rebellion
To be dating Bev
Because even in a city that is majority Asian
Some people see Charlie everywhere
Equate immigrant with enemy
Don't understand
There are multiple sides to every conflict
And who were her grandparents?
Nationalists
Loyalists
Farmers
Landowners
The people the Vietcong accused
Of exploiting their own people
Bev once told me a story
Of how when she was a little girl
On a rainy day
On a family trip to Vietnam
She stood in front of a bronze statue of Ho Chi Minh
And flicked it off with both fingers

Yelling,
"You ruined my country!"

On dusty afternoons in Chihuahua
My great grandmother
Would put my grandmother into a laundry basket
Cramp her limbs inside the weave or burlap
To hide her away from soldiers
During the Revolution
My grandmother married a hotel owner
And they fled to El Paso
My great uncle left with them
To avoid fighting in the Mexican Revolution
Later
He returned to Mexico
To avoid fighting for the United States in WWI.

Refugees
Can come from multiple sides of every conflict
And whether their story is epic
Tragic
Or somewhat farcical
Often depends on who's telling the story.

I didn't date Bev
Because her grandparents
Supported Ngo Dinh Diem
Or I support Ho Chi Minh
I dated Bev
Because of the punch of her jokes
The fullness of her laugh
The comfortable weight of her body on mine
A body once exposed
Black hair and auburn eyes
Pale skin
In the open air
As I laid on a blanket
In a rain gutter
Shaded by pines
On a cliff overlooking the 57.

Batman Rides Shotgun with Barbie

Batman
Drove Barbie's red Corvette
Because what use did Ken have for it?
I found Mattel red plastic
Tucked away in a corner of my sister's room
This Corvette
A perfect open-aired ride with detailed wheels and hubcaps
Friends would come over
And while younger
They wouldn't question it
But as the years passed
More of them would ask,
"Isn't that for girls?"
My father drove our family
Would often comment on my mother's driving
Suggest it was dangerous
Even though she's only been in one accident
Her entire life
But dad was the breadwinner
Mom earned like she drove
More
On the side
I've never followed an order from a boss who was a woman
Like I've never gone through a quick lane change
On the freeway
Riding shotgun
Without second-guessing it
I'm a sexist
I've never said "boss"
Without feeling the need to add "woman"
To codify
Like how some people
Can't help but specify
That "the jerk" they ran into at the store was
"Black"
"Hispanic"

"Asian"
Other
Because
"Well
You know
How THEY are"
And that this is all much worse
When the identities of race and gender
Intersected
I wish that when I said "boss"
It wasn't a straight white man that came to mind
Even though most of my bosses have been women
I wish that I wouldn't find the need to second-guess them
That I could look up to my bosses
Imagine their career path
Their story
Their ambition
Their struggle
See their good qualities
Admire their professionalism
Aspire to be more like them
I wish that the line between me and them
Wasn't as sharp as that between Batman and Barbie
I wish that I didn't have to throw that red Corvette away
Because some idiot told me that it was "for girls"
I wish that those jerks at Mattel
Hadn't told generations of young women
That the only car in the toy line
Belonged to Ken
That it was up to a man to drive them
To give them money
You are assertive
Not bossy
Bold
Not dangerous
Open
Not emotional
Adaptable
Not irrational

They pay you an unequal wage
To keep the wheel in their hands
The keys in their pockets
But screw a glass ceiling
You were meant to drive a convertible
That check
That raise
Those benefits
Equal pay
They are yours
You already know that
You don't need me to tell you
It's more for me
To come to terms with
To stop being such a chauvinist
It's time we stopped looking in the rearview
But instead
Towards the road ahead
I never liked Ken
He can ride in the backseat
And for a change
Let the kids play
I'd like to see Batman ride shotgun
With Barbie.

Bucky

When I was young
I had a sidekick
Her name was Bucky
Bucky was my fourth-grade friend
Standing out there
Waiting for me
On my fourth-grade lawn
My mom was glad
I didn't have many friends back then
Bucky stood
With an ugly puffy pink jacket
And a bowl cut
That seemed the wet dream
Of every model minority stereotype
But Bucky didn't want to hit the books
Didn't want to apply for the Ivy League
Before she became a woman
She didn't want to be
Known for getting As in her classes
No, Bucky wanted to be a superhero
Or at least a sidekick
So we went on trips together
Caped crusaders
Our on our way to the comic book store
For what could be considered our first date
Bucky told me that she
Wanted "to know everything
About the X-Men"
Bucky wanted to be my girlfriend
I was too stupid to understand
Or, at least pretended not to
Bucky hung up her cape
Left the superhero game
Started looking to other places
Other friends
For attention

Years later
Bucky
Was on the side of drugs
Booze
Piercings
And tattoos
Partially in the name of her own personal liberation
But also
Because she was addicted
Bucky became the sidekick
To supervillains
Like Harley Quinn
They kicked her in her face
They kicked her
To keep her in place
Like a gang initiation
They jumped her in
And Bucky emerged a real bad bitch
She was my hero
The toughest of people
Can fool you into forgetting
They're often the most hurt inside
And Bucky learned well that
When you wear a mask
No one can see you cry
My powers included
An icy cold stare of judgment
When
Maybe
Really
Bucky just wanted a friend again
I was too stupid to understand
Or, at least chose not too
Superman leaps tall buildings
Spider-man swings his webs through New York City
I had the power to turn my back
On one of my oldest friends
Years passed
And extra, extra

Read all about it
They told me
Bucky was the victim of sexual assault
They told me,
"Bucky was raped"
The news came in
And I didn't know what to say
Comic books don't teach you
How to reconnect with old friends
How to talk to them again
How to listen to them
How to help them feel loved
How to help them learn how to trust
A man again
Anyone
Supervillains kill millions
But they never do anything as evil
As sexually assaulting someone
Anyone
One of your childhood crushes
One of your childhood friends
And superheroes
Would have never turned their backs
On Bucky
A woman
Who deserved much more
Than being a sidekick
To anyone.

Sean

I wanted to be like you Sean.

I wanted to be a leader like you were
I wanted to be able to gather up a group
As quickly as you could
You managed to get all of us
To ride our bikes
Into the sunset
And long after.

I wanted to be able to break my bones like you could
You pushed your bike up ramps
Haphazardly constructed
The previous weekend
You rode your bike into the street
Flying in the wrong direction
Fell onto the asphalt
Hard and gritty
You did this continuously
Cheating death so often
For you
Pain was just another ramp to ride
Another challenge to meet
Head down
Arms out.

You were stupid Sean
You deserved every broken bone
But, as a kid, I would jealously watch you
From my upstairs window
Reading, doing homework
I watched you
Bleed your signature
All over the goddamned street
And sometimes when I look between the blinds
I'll still think I'm going to see you

Riding
Screaming and cursing
On your bike
Scooter
Or skateboard.

I hate you
But I can't seem to figure out why
I wish I had a memory
Something to point to
A time when you convinced the other kids to beat me up
Or days and days of calling me names
Something to clearly explain
How our friendship changed
And why it fills me with disgust to think about you to this day.

Instead
I remember how playing with you at ten
Was like having one adventure after another
Bringing each cut
And bruised arm
To show off to my dad
And frustrate my mother
I would smile, "I have friends"
And that, meant a lot to me back then.

I remember us as commandos
G.I. Joes
On our next mission
Jumping fences
Crawling under them
To cross the backyards that separated our houses
Avoiding our neighbors' dogs
Clipping at our heels
And that is where we would stop in a stranger's house
Build our fort
We each claimed a bush or a tree
And had a pinecone war!

Why do I hate you, Sean?
I think it was because you changed
Or, maybe, because you refused to change
Like how you refused to realize
That just acting like you knew everything
Without bothering to learn anything
Wasn't enough
Like how I would leave town
And come back
After months and months
And you were still at the local bar
Hanging around and scrounging
For favors and action
Like a man searching through piles of cigarette butts.

Sean
Your parents seemed to love
To buy you
Everything you ever wanted
But you refused to appreciate
How great your life actually was
You died so close to the street you may have hated
But you weren't able to ride your bike
Scooter
Or car
Away from—

A car crash
And Sean's gone.

Jeremiah

There were only a handful of black kids
In my hometown growing up
There was Alden
Who was a mean brother
Whether on the tetherball or
The handball court
Who, years later
After discovering improv
And drama in high school
Told me I had the makings of a Columbine killer
There was Jamal
Who was a Pop Warner
And high school star athlete
Felt the pressure choking down on him to be that
From his friends and family
Until sometime in college he decided to grow his hair out
Pick up a guitar and declare to people at kickbacks,
"I'm white now"
There was Medusa
Who
With a name like that
Never really had a chance
There was Karen
Who was a casual friend
In the early years of elementary
But my friend Frank and I were so racist
We couldn't imagine playing X-Men
With Karen as any other character but Storm.

Then there was Jeremiah
Jeremiah who was the coolest kid in school
By the time he was in the fifth grade
He seemed to have accumulated
The life experience of a High School Senior
Jeremiah and I never really crossed paths until the day we both met Taylor
Taylor was a white girl from Utah

Mormon
But even then
A real spitfire
Jeremiah really liked that about her
And I don't know why I was there on the playground
When Jeremiah met the "new girl" for the first time
But there I was
We went on the swings
Down the slides
And sometimes when I walk that path
I can hear three sets of footsteps echoing
Can hear Jeremiah asking Taylor to let him walk her home
He asked her if she knew what scamming meant
I can still hear Taylor turning him down.

Jeremiah had a cousin in middle school named Jameson
He had thin and short dreadlocks parted down the middle
And wore white wifebeaters
Jameson was always smirking
He was always making fun of me and everything
But I never really minded
The first day he met me
He asked Jeremiah,
"Why you hangin' with this white boy?"
And Jeremiah said,
"Nah, he ain't white
He's Mexican or something"
And Jameson said,
"Nah, he white"
And one day I followed them both back
Up the hill and around the block
To a one-story house
With overgrown hedges in place of walls or fences
And Jameson smirked at me
Before inviting me in
And Jeremiah looked at us both
And said,
"Nah"
He pushed me back

Looked me in the eyes and said,
"Go home"
That's probably the last time I talked to him.

I would walk by that house alone or with my bike
Sometimes there was shouting inside
The silhouettes in the front window got loud
And Jeremiah fought with Jameson
I wonder if he was still smirking when he hit him
Sometimes I would walk by
Maybe hear their grandmother
And the evidence of good times in that house too
But either way
It was none of my business.

Winter

New Year's Day

The world is new and cold
Naked and pointy trees tell the tale
Almost as bare as those mountains north
Condensation on car windows
The defrost button once a stranger
Now a friend
To drive is to risk being lost in the fog
To walk is to risk being stuck in the rain
Rain here brings snow on mountains
A little produces rings on ledges
Like the icing on layers of cake
Like rings of tinsel on your tree
You just packed that into the garage
Yesterday
Scarves, mittens, and umbrellas rush to the mall
The hubcaps of white SUVs ride to the mountains
Snowboarding and ski trips
You mostly stay home
Pretend to enjoy the solemnity of the gray world
But actually hate it
Hate the world in shadow
The only thing you enjoy is that stinging cold outside
Before you break a sweat
Cutting wood and gathering kindling
Before you flick your lighter
To begin your night's entertainment
Outside with that dark blue and purple sky
And the black silhouettes of the few trees seen from your backyard
Tonight
Rain will wash you out
Tomorrow
You will love the smell of your house filled with the memory of smoke
Today
You will meet your friend Mario at a coffeeshop
Layer-up to sit outside in cold metal chairs
Under an awning and clear skies

The mountains will be covered with snow
One of you will remark how that's a rare sight
The other will agree
Indeed
You are two Southern Californians
Shivering
Playing at Winter.

I Wept and Howled that Night

I wept and howled that night
After you left
Shaking
Repeating,
"I don't want to die alone
I don't want to die alone"
What started as a chant
Became unintelligible
As each syllable was stretched
Into phonemes of fear and admission
Pure animal religion
Helplessness in flooded eyeballs
Streams of mucous
And panicked breath
I caught it
When I said to myself
"Get to work—
When this is over
You'll feel better
You'll work anyways
Gotta work every day
Get it over with
You might as well start now"
And I pushed it down
Into my stomach
Or somewhere else inside
Contemplated a drink
To break years of sobriety
You weren't worth it
Had a cigarette instead
It ended a week without
In a mutual pledge to quit
And all that panic
Became a familiar ache
The drive in me
To become something great

To show you
To show everyone
It was the same as always
Within minutes
I sat on that bed
Atop sheets that still held your scent
And I sent out booking emails.

I Am the One Who Knocks

In a world of poets
Waiting for doors to be opened
I am the one who knocks
Knock, knock
I said,
Knock, knock
Who's there?
Son of parents from Boyle Heights and East Los Angeles
First in his family to graduate from college
Travels the country
With the title "professional spoken word artist"
Knock, knock
Who's there?
The local kid made good
The passionate poet with a twinkle in his eye
And a song in his step
He kept doodling
In the coloring book of his memories
To fulfill those childhood dreams of making it
Knock, knock
Who's there?
Fiery Mexican poet
Advocate for social justice
Knock, knock
Who's there?
Recovering alcoholic
Moves forward with life
After struggle with addiction
Knock, knock
Who's there?
The kid who pissed his pants
In the fourth grade
Who picked his nose and ate his mocos
Who licked bricks in the backyard
Because he liked the taste
Knock, knock

Who's there?
A joke
Joker
Charlatan
Opportunist
Impostor
But, hey
You've got to fake it until you make it
You keep building a foundation
Stack the accomplishments
And at some point the mundane
Finally becomes the sacred
You know who I think is a joke?
Knock, knock
Who's there?
Waiting
Waiting, who?
Everyone who's waiting in the wings
For the curtain to be lifted up
For the doors to be opened
For someone to let them in the backdoor
Take them backstage
Most doors get slammed in your face
Most keys to the kingdom
Remained fastened to the waist
Try to please the gatekeepers
Have fun spending years
Polishing the gates
Knock, knock
Who's there?
The idiot who believes in knocking
The underdog story
Because the people say they love an underdog story
Because they say they love hard work
And I put in work
I don't wait for doors to be opened
I use the internet
I find the doors
And I knock

And when I get rejected?
I find myself something to hide behind
Allow myself to tear up for a bit
And then I walk
Over to the next house
And again, I knock
So, you can't mock the struggle
And you can't knock my hustle
Knock, knock
Knock, knock
Knock, knock
Who's there?
MEEEEEEE!!!
Your heart
Your mind
Your wallet
OPEN UP!!!

In 30

Hopes and regrets
My phone and late-night cigarettes
In 30 or 10
It's time to come in
Set the alarm
Head against the pillow
Sleep comes
Or
I spend the night worrying.

Alarm rings
It's morning
Turn the lights on
It's still dark outside
Brew the coffee
Drink while last-minute-packing
Grab the luggage
Call a rideshare
In 30 we get there
Have a conversation
Just to get the body going
Wave goodbye at the airport terminal
Smoking
Automatic glass doors
Self-service kiosk
Get the tickets
Turn down the upgrades
Stand in the line going all the way
From security to baggage claim
Chew some gum
Pinch my index with my thumb
It's too hard sometimes
Stuck between waist-high bars and rope
In a sea of folks
Making eye contact
Brushing up against bodies

We're all travelers in purgatory
At the podium
Homeland scans my ID
Does the double-take
"Yup, that's me"
Already took my belt off
Unzipped my sweater
Security becomes a highly choreographed dance
And every time
I only get better
Some jerk slows up the process
Misses the obvious
I strike a pose
They wave me through
Or pull me over for bag inspection
See if my books might be weapons
I'm not into hyperbole like some other poets
They aren't
A seat to put myself back together
My keys
And my wallet
Chew more gum
It snaps with the popping of the package
Try to find the most isolated seat
Encircle my luggage
Fire up the laptop
Connect to Wi-Fi
Jack the headphones in
Some private time
Watch the monitors
I'm often one of the last to board the plane
In no hurry for the walk of shame
Have a seat
Next to
Babies or kids?
Some sterling conversationalists?
Who might I be trapped in this death can in the sky
For hours with?
Take out my phone

Turn it off
Or into airplane mode
Crack open a good old-fashioned paper book
Read while we taxi
Head against my seat when we takeoff
Hopes and regrets
A few hours before we touchdown
Then
A cigarette
Sleep comes
Or
I spend the next 30 worrying.

Room 108

Room 108
Is brown
Beige
And green
Motel room
Ugly wallpaper
A table
Bathroom
Two beds
Queens
Room 108
Has 5 lights
But was made to be dark
Black
With lights off
And 2 silhouettes
In Room 108
A set of teeth gleam white
Another stained yellow
These 2 silhouettes
Writhing in pain and pleasure
It's been said earlier
Outside
Not in Room 108
That racism is very real
But race isn't
It's a construct like
4 walls
Concrete
Plaster
Wood
Ugly wallpaper
A table
Bathroom
Two beds
And racism

It suffocates
It pinches
It pulls
It slaps
It slashes our backs
And people
In the dark
Have no use for it
But who are we kidding?
I am more moonlight reflection
Creeping in from the edges of curtains
Covering windows
Than shadow
And there's something about that
She likes
Screams out
Something about me
Something about white
I want to say
I am not the son of Jefferson
I want to remind her
That I am a Mexican
But Room 108
Is a construct
And fetish can be pleasure
And the truth
Is the kind of thing that can scare it all away.

I'd Like to Be

Driftwood
Wrangled, scarred, and polished
Under a thunderhead sky
Past the reach of settled land
Where the grass grows thin
And the pines lean
Sparse
I'd like to be
Cocktail napkins
Podiums and people gathered
Glossy trifold brochures folded with
A name and picture
Your speaker
Better yet
Invisible
Your sponsor and donor
I'd like to be
A megaphone
Filled with grime and righteousness
A used and tattered army jacket
That's seen its share of arrests
That has felt the cold floor of jail cells
For only the right reasons
A life
Miserable
But with few compromises.

Because I Could Not Stop for Money

Because I could not stop for Money
She kindly stopped for me
The limo held but just ourselves—
Fame, Fortune, and Glory
A black carriage
With immaculate rims and tinted glass
Stretching into Eternity.

Money and I cruised by the corner
Where poets cyphered their poems
Long after the conclusion of the evening's open mic
The poets stood there
As I once had
Trading metaphors for similes
Under the dim lights
And onward
We passed locked gates
Into the land of grand estates
Once, I had sat at the foot of the mountain
Looking up
Now, looking down
The nighttime sea
Golden, twinkling lights below
I felt like I owned the night
Wondered,
"Is this what being on top of the world feels like?"
Felt my pen strike
Like my hand had signed—
Wait, what did I sign?
Money assured me,
"I'll never put any limit
On what you write"
Soon, there were cameras
And I smiled for the cameras
Performed for the cameras
But, fell out of favor of the cameras

Money said, "Come on, do the one that I like!
You know, the one that gets the crowd hyped?"
So, I did it
All was flashes
Performance to performance
Crowds flocked to purchase
Rep' the network
Rep' the label
Millions of artists
All packaged and labeled
I don't know when I first
Put my hands up against the plastic
I don't know when I first
Realized I was trapped in my package
Money had made me into something
Cheap and disgusting
Something to hang on a shelf
Or packed into a box
No artist
Just some kind of product
The price of my integrity
Plastered over my chest
Since then
It's been
Hindsight
20/20
"You should've known
When dealing with Money"
But all things aside
The years on the inside
Have been alright
When all your points of articulation
Are as amiable as an action figure's to the whims of others
It's easy to adjust to life
There was only
That one
Lonely
Guilty
Night

It was in the store
Hanging on the rack
As the lights flickered off
It was when I first realized
I could never again hope to rejoin those poets
Still trading metaphors for similes
Under the dim lights.

Your Life is a Landscape

Right now
You're in your life
Grounded
In the thick of it
Thinking about
Moving forward
You know where you need to go
But all you can see is each obstacle in front of you
Each tree, signpost, ditch, and building
And even when your field is clear in all directions
You still carry heavy baggage in your arms
On your shoulders
The weight of it can hold you in place.

Imagine instead
You're looking out a window
A large landscape before you
Plains, ponds, mountains, rivers, and valleys
The sprawl of cities
You're 7.5 miles up in the sky
What you see is your life
Look to your right
The limit is what you can remember
Look to your left
That's your future
Everything between
Is everything you've ever done
Everything you've ever been
Everywhere you've ever gone
And everything that's ever happened to you.

You see that marsh down there?
You remember how scared you were
To be stuck in that mud
To flail your arms and legs
To scream for help

To think it could be the end of your journey
But you're not there
You're 7.5 miles up in the sky
Remember?
You're looking out a window
A large landscape before you
And that marsh is a tiny detail
You can see how you got in there
The steps you took to get out
Perhaps, most importantly
You can see all of the places you could've gone instead.

You see that mountain?
You remember how hard it was to climb
The pain in your legs
The ache in your back
Each labored breath
How good it felt to be on top
It was bittersweet even then
Knowing you would have to come down
Was that mountain part of a range?
Or, was it a single feature on the landscape?
But, no matter what surrounds
Or, what is to come
You see that the peak you stood upon
Will always remain
A place to see
A place to remember
To remind you of that of which you are capable.

Still, worry fills you
Whenever you try to look ahead
Straining to get a better view forward through this window
You hit some turbulence
What dark clouds
What dangerous skies
You look down
Upon the landscape of your life
You realize this is what it has been without

You see the effects of a drought
When the storm comes
Some trees and developments will be cleared
And new life will take root
After the rain falls.

And what if there was no limit to this window?
That the steady march of this flight
Didn't determine what you could see of your life?
That this wasn't just a better view of what was to come
But that it was already there, all along?
That you could see it all?
The streets are paved
The paths are cleared
The footprints and track marks are already there
But, so is the sun
The moon
The darkness
And stars
The feeling of touch
The smells in the air.

The river will carry
Though you know how deep
The current will take you
Though you know where it leads
The water is still wet
And you won't be able to entirely repress your fear
The next time you come close to drowning.

You're in your life
But you can see out of it
You can have perspective
Even when you're grounded
Don't focus on trying to see immediately forward
For your advantage
It would be like trying to map out a forest
While running into a tree
As you take in your life's landscape

Remember that there is no limit to what is there
But, there are limits to where you will go
And what you can perceive.

You have traveled
You do travel
You will travel
And there are all of those places to travel to
The entirety of your life's landscape is before you.

When you get off the plane
The baggage will still remain
But you can set it down
Pull back the zippers and look inside
You carry with you
That marsh, those clouds, that mountain
How amazing they should all fit together into those packages!
You laugh at that
Pick your life up
And it all feels so much lighter
You keep moving.

Familiar Ghosts

The Diamond Bar Ranch is long gone
But cattle still graze on dawn's meadow
In Chino Hills they roam
Fireworks dash upwards
Illuminating Bucky's face
On a Fourth of July night at Paul C. Grow
When I leave Diamond Bar
I want to go back there
Because other places
Are full of only lonely roads and unfamiliar ghosts
Some say,
"This town is dead"
But it's here where I get to keep mine close.

Say a Prayer for Me

Say a prayer for me
That when the wind calls
And the 286 comes
That I'll rise up from this bench
And take it
Say a prayer for me
That when these doors close
I'll finally be able to let go
Of these ghosts
That I'll be able to crawl out of this house
Shaped like my mother's womb
Get up on my own two feet
And keep walking
Say a prayer for me
As this bus takes off
That when it's time for me to finally take care of her
And not just tell the lie
I'm used to telling others
That I'll stay through the most painful moments
Like she did for my dad
Or when she drove me to court
Or when she picked me up from jail
Say a prayer for me
As the bus jolts
That I stay steady enough
Through these days
To never pick the bottle back up
To understand
That in life
It is possible to change
And to grow
But to remember
That there are still some things about us
That we can't control
Say a prayer for me
As I move to find my seat in the back

That I'll finally pay you back
Those friends of friends
Who put up a collection
To help cover my medical expenses
Say a prayer for me
As I put my head up against the window
That the next time I sit down at the casino
Anxiously stacking and shuffling chips
I'll remember every dollar
That brought me closer to visiting my nieces
And how many months I went without seeing them
Say a prayer for me
When the distortion rings
And the guitar strums
And the 286 departs in a cloud of smoke...

I want to thank you for always being there
I want to thank you for staying through the seasons
Thank you for always watching
I would say a prayer for you
But we both know I'm too damned selfish.

Give me the strength to change the things I can
And to accept the things I can't.

Say a prayer for me.

About the Author

David A. Romero is a Mexican-American spoken word artist from Diamond Bar, CA. Romero is the co-founder and editor-in-chief of El Martillo Press. Romero is the author of *My Name Is Romero* (FlowerSong Press 2020), *Diamond Bars 2* (Moon Tide Press, 2024) and *Diamond Bars: The Street Version* (Dimlights Publishing, 2010). Romero has received honorariums from nearly a hundred colleges and universities in thirty-four different states in the USA and has performed live in Mexico, Italy, and France. Romero's work has been published in literary magazines in the United States, Mexico, England, Scotland, Canada and Hungary. Romero has opened for Latin Grammy winning bands Ozomatli and La Santa Cecilia. Romero's work has been published in anthologies alongside poets laureate Joy Harjo, Lawrence Ferlinghetti, Luis J. Rodriguez, Jack Hirschman, and Tongo Eisen-Martin. Romero has won the Uptown Slam at the historic Green Mill in Chicago; the birthplace of slam poetry. Romero offers a scholarship for high school seniors interested in spoken word and social justice: "The Romero Scholarship for Excellence in Spoken Word." Find him at davidaromero.com & elmartillopress.com

Acknowledgements

"You Were Born a Tree" published in *Reimagine America (An Anthology for the Future)*, VAGABOND, 2022, nominated for a Pushcart Prize.

"Basketball with Edgar Allan Poe" published in *ARTNOIS Magazine*, August 2013. "Batman Rides Shotgun with Barbie" published in *Label Me Latina/o* Spring 2021 Volume XI. "The Redemption of Roxy Salgado" published by *Somos en Escrito*, March, 2022. "A Neighborhood of Glass Windows," "A Safe Place to Live," "The 286," "Summer at the Movies," and "It Washes Us Away" published by *Life in Quarantine: Witnessing Global Pandemic*, Poetic Media Lab and Center for Spatial and Textual Analysis (CESTA) at Stanford University, June 2022. "Bucky" published in *The Los Angeles Press*, Volume 8 "The Chain," June 2023. *"I'd Like to Be"* and *"Familiar Ghosts"* published in *1749*, April 2024 and *"New Year's Day"* published in *1749*, June 2024.

***

This book is dedicated to my sister Julie. It's true: when I was little, one of her favorite ways to spoil me as my big sister was to buy me popcorn and soda and take me to the movies. Back then, there was an AMC movie theater in Puente Hills, that's closed now, on the other side of the 60 from the newer megaplex, that she liked to take me to. Julie took me to see both animated and live action movies. She would listen to me talk about the movies on the way home afterwards as well as about novels and comic books. When I went through my intense Edgar Allan Poe phase in fourth grade, Julie would sometimes listen to me recite his poems and read his short stories. One or two of her friends got a kick out of it too. Julie and her friends were some of my earliest audiences. To this day, Julie will invite some of her friends and coworkers to my readings and book signings. Thank you again, Julie.

Thank you to Mr. Kirkeby (I'll always know him as that) for writing this book's foreword. For those unaware, Mr. Kirkeby is one of the most accomplished teachers in the history of Diamond Bar. He's a multiple "Teacher of the Year" award-winner. And while there is no statue or plaque dedicated to him (yet), he carried a reputation as an educator such that parents and students would talk extensively about him and their chances of getting into his classes. My sister Julie sang his praises for years (and still does). I was nervous and excited to take AP English with him. From his costumed performances of poems and essays to his in-depth lectures and drawings on Transcendentalism and other literary and philosophical movements, to his occasionally scathing reviews of our student projects and essays, it was apparent to generations of his pupils that Mr. Kirkeby operated on an entirely different level from other teachers. I've met many professors over the years, and in my opinion, Mr. Kirkeby could've taught at some of the most prestigious universities in the world, such was his talent as an educator, and so compelling was his love of literature, and yet, we were lucky enough to have him in Diamond Bar.

Special thanks go out to Rachel Khong, author of the recently released *Real Americans: a novel* and *Goodbye, Vitamin,* who, wouldn't you know it, was in one or two of those aforementioned AP English classes taught by Mr. Kirkeby. I remember Rachel's infectious optimism, her precision as a storyteller, and the fact that she was kind enough to give me a copy of Miles Davis' *Kind of Blue*, which remains one of my favorite albums (and especially one I enjoy listening to while I write).

Tacos go out to Gustavo Arellano, legendary columnist and journalist, who dared to follow up his wildly popular and influential collection of essays, *Ask A Mexican, with Orange County: A Personal History,* diving into the public history of the OC while also explaining his and his family's connection to its cities and neighborhoods. He opened my eyes to the Spanish and Mexican history behind suburbia in SoCal, and perhaps more importantly, that as a writer it was worth taking a chance to write about one's home and the mixed feelings that might provoke, even if others might prefer that you stick to the topics that you're known for. This book wouldn't exist without Gustavo and his bravery.

I'd like to thank my friends that I grew up with, some as far back as elementary school, through middle, and especially high school, that have remained in my life through the decades. Chief among them, Gene, Brandon, and Brett (but, Ryan, Matt, Kenta, Anthony, and those unnamed, I have love for you, too). So many in-jokes and stories. We've watched movies together, listened to music together, talked about books together, and have philosophized for hours on-end over cups of coffee and cigarettes, and yes, over bottles and glasses too, for a time. We're getting older now, and despite me always being broke and sometimes being stuck in a rut that must make it hard for me to spend a lot of time with, I want to thank you for keeping me in your lives: calling me over the phone, sending text messages, telling me about your families and inviting me to your weddings and such. It's an honor to know you and your families.

I want to thank my best friend, and co-founder of El Martillo Press: Matt Sedillo, for hanging in there with me during a tough time in my life, in the middle of the pandemic, when I was working at a restaurant supply store, and had all but given up on poetry. As I wrote about in an article published by *LA Taco*, it was a time when I constantly had nightmares about stacks of pallets and towers of PPE materials crashing over my head. I was concerned with delivery schedules and bills of lading and how much my supervisors might chew me out on any given day. Matt's dreams, his recent successes with FlowerSong Press, and his prodding for me to pick back up the pen inspired me to write this book. Matt and I would meet up before I started my shift, sit in his kitchen, and write poems for hours, stopping to share what we had written, me working on this book and him working on *City on the Second Floor*. We competed to see who could write poems the fastest. I dug into an old notebook that I had put together in high school labeled "Ideas" that I've kept all these years and started to turn what once had been outlines for movie scripts into many of the poems in this collection. He said it was cheating, but he still managed to finish his manuscript first.

Thanks to my El Martillo Press familia, to my FlowerSong Press pressmates, and again, to some of the first poets and writers to have supported me on my poetic journey, Poetri, Besskepp, Lee Ballinger, Mark Lipman, David "Judah1" Oliver and Brian "SuperB" Oliva.

Thank you to Moon Tide Press Editor-in-Chief Eric Morago for selecting *Diamond Bars 2* and to Moon Tide Press Marketing Specialist Ellen Webre for championing my work.

Thank you to day job coworkers and supervisors Cody, Troy, Carlos, Serpas, Juan, Comanche, Mike, Trevor, Ivan, and more, who have sweat and bled beside me, showed me the ropes, and were always (well, maybe not always) ready to pitch in a "shovel" and help dig me out of a difficult situation or two.

Finally, I want to acknowledge writers, performers, and creators who inspired this book: Bill Waterson, Dr. Seuss, Gustavo Arellano, Edgar Allan Poe, Emily Dickinson, Rod Serling, Alvin Schwartz, Kevin Smith, Slug of Atmosphere, Sufjan Stevens, Paul Simon, George Lucas, Jon Favreau, Henry David Thoreau, Bradley Nowell, Jack Kerouac, Bob Dylan, David Mickey Evans, Kurt Vonnegut, Virginia Woolf, Luis Buñuel, Jim Lee, Todd McFarlane, Jack Johnson, Jason Aldean, Frank Turner, Mos Def, Mitch Hedberg, George Lopez, Pablo Francisco, Ted Chiang, Neil deGrasse Tyson, and to all of those 90s one-hit-wonders like Sponge, Paperboy, Less Than Jake, Lil Rob, and the Sneaker Pimps whose singles still give me goosebumps and instantly take me back to times and places long gone.

Also Available from Moon Tide Press

Dissection Day, Ally McGregor (2023)
He's a Color Until He's Not, Christian Hanz Lozada (2023)
The Language of Fractions, Nicelle Davis (2023)
Paradise Anonymous, Oriana Ivy (2023)
Now You Are a Missing Person, Susan Hayden (2023)
Maze Mouth, Brian Sonia-Wallace (2023)
Tangled by Blood, Rebecca Evans (2023)
Another Way of Loving Death, Jeremy Ra (2023)
Kissing the Wound, J.D. Isip (2023)
Feed It to the River, Terhi K. Cherry (2022)
Beat Not Beat: An Anthology of California Poets Screwing
    on the Beat and Post-Beat Tradition (2022)
When There Are Nine: Poems Celebrating the Life an
Achievements of Ruth Bader Ginsburg (2022)
The Knife Thrower's Daughter, Terri Niccum (2022)
2 Revere Place, Aruni Wijesinghe (2022)
Here Go the Knives, Kelsey Bryan-Zwick (2022)
Trumpets in the Sky, Jerry Garcia (2022)
Threnody, Donna Hilbert (2022)
A Burning Lake of Paper Suns, Ellen Webre (2021)
Instructions for an Animal Body, Kelly Gray (2021)
Head *V* Heart: New & Selected Poems, Rob Sturma (2021)
Sh!t Men Say to Me: A Poetry Anthology in Response
    to Toxic Masculinity (2021)
Flower Grand First, Gustavo Hernandez (2021)
Everything is Radiant Between the Hates, Rich Ferguson (2020)
When the Pain Starts: Poetry as Sequential Art,
    Alan Passman (2020)
This Place Could Be Haunted If I Didn't Believe in Love,
    Lincoln McElwee (2020)
Impossible Thirst, Kathryn de Lancellotti (2020)
Lullabies for End Times, Jennifer Bradpiece (2020)
Crabgrass World, Robin Axworthy (2020)
Contortionist Tongue, Dania Ayah Alkhouli (2020)
The only thing that makes sense is to grow, Scott Ferry (2020)
Dead Letter Box, Terri Niccum (2019)

Tea and Subtitles: Selected Poems 1999-2019,
    Michael Miller (2019)
At the Table of the Unknown, Alexandra Umlas (2019)
The Book of Rabbits, Vince Trimboli (2019)
Everything I Write Is a Love Song to the World,
    David McIntire (2019)
Letters to the Leader, HanaLena Fennel (2019)
Darwin's Garden, Lee Rossi (2019)
Dark Ink: A Poetry Anthology Inspired by Horror (2018)
Drop and Dazzle, Peggy Dobreer (2018)
Junkie Wife, Alexis Rhone Fancher (2018)
The Moon, My Lover, My Mother, & the Dog,
    Daniel McGinn (2018)
Lullaby of Teeth: An Anthology of Southern California
    Poetry (2017)
Angels in Seven, Michael Miller (2016)
A Likely Story, Robbi Nester (2014)
Embers on the Stairs, Ruth Bavetta (2014)
The Green of Sunset, John Brantingham (2013)
The Savagery of Bone, Timothy Matthew Perez (2013)
The Silence of Doorways, Sharon Venezio (2013)
Cosmos: An Anthology of Southern California Poetry (2012)
Straws and Shadows, Irena Praitis (2012)
In the Lake of Your Bones, Peggy Dobreer (2012)
I Was Building Up to Something, Susan Davis (2011)
Hopeless Cases, Michael Kramer (2011)
One World, Gail Newman (2011)
What We Ache For, Eric Morago (2010)
Now and Then, Lee Mallory (2009)
Pop Art: An Anthology of Southern California Poetry (2009)
In the Heaven of Never Before, Carine Topal (2008)
A Wild Region, Kate Buckley (2008)
Carving in Bone: An Anthology of Orange County Poetry (2007)
Kindness from a Dark God, Ben Trigg (2007)
A Thin Strand of Lights, Ricki Mandeville (2006)
Sleepyhead Assassins, Mindy Nettifee (2006)
Tide Pools: An Anthology of Orange County Poetry (2006)
Lost American Nights: Lyrics & Poems, Michael Ubaldini (2006)

Patrons

Moon Tide Press would like to thank the following people for their support in helping publish the finest poetry from the Southern California region. To sign up as a patron, visit www.moontidepress.com or send an email to publisher@moontidepress.com.

Anonymous
Robin Axworthy
Conner Brenner
Nicole Connolly
Bill Cushing
Susan Davis
Kristen Baum DeBeasi
Peggy Dobreer
Kate Gale
Dennis Gowans
Alexis Rhone Fancher
HanaLena Fennel
Half Off Books & Brad T. Cox
Donna Hilbert
Jim & Vicky Hoggatt
Michael Kramer
Ron Koertge & Bianca Richards
Gary Jacobelly
Ray & Christi Lacoste
Jeffery Lewis
Zachary & Tammy Locklin
Lincoln McElwee
David McIntire
José Enrique Medina

Michael Miller & Rachanee Srisavasdi
Michelle & Robert Miller
Ronny & Richard Morago
Terri Niccum
Andrew November
Jeremy Ra
Luke & Mia Salazar
Jennifer Smith
Roger Sponder
Andrew Turner
Rex Wilder
Mariano Zaro
Wes Bryan Zwick